# WILBUR, THE MIRACLE PIG

# WILBUR, THE MIRACLE PIG

By Linda Zirzow

Illustrated by
Gretchen Burmeister
Avon Lake, OHIO

XULON PRESS ELITE

Xulon Press Elite
2301 Lucien Way #415
Maitland, FL 32751
407.339.4217
www.xulonpress.com

© 2021 by Linda Zirzow

All rights reserved solely by the author. The author guarantees all contents are original and do not infringe upon the legal rights of any other person or work. No part of this book may be reproduced in any form without the permission of the author.

Due to the changing nature of the Internet, if there are any web addresses, links, or URLs included in this manuscript, these may have been altered and may no longer be accessible. The views and opinions shared in this book belong solely to the author and do not necessarily reflect those of the publisher. The publisher therefore disclaims responsibility for the views or opinions expressed within the work.

Unless otherwise indicated, Scripture quotations taken from the Holy Bible, New International Version (NIV). Copyright © 1973, 1978, 1984, 2011 by Biblica, Inc.™. Used by permission. All rights reserved.

Paperback ISBN-13: 978-1-66283-103-4
Ebook ISBN-13: 978-1-66283-104-1

# Introduction

On Labor Day of 2011, I broke my hip at a party which resulted in almost a year of physical therapy.

While at one of my therapy sessions, I observed a young boy, maybe six or seven, who was not doing at all well with his physical therapy. I asked my physical therapist if I could talk to the little boy. After the therapist heard the story that I told the little boy, the therapist said that I should put the story on paper. My intentions are to have copies in the physical therapy areas for young people.

As a result, I followed up, and <u>Wilbur, the Miracle Pig</u>, became paper.

Everyone has heard of Old McDonald who had a farm. Once upon a time, there was another farmer named Frank. He and his wife, Darline, had a daughter, Linda. They all lived on a farm in Illinois.

On the farm were cows, pigs, chickens, ducks, turkeys, sheep, guineas, and geese. Linda loved all the animals, and they loved her. She would spend a lot of time in the barn petting the chickens, calves, piglets, and lambs.

One day, Linda was in the barn and walked by the pig pen. She heard her father say aloud, "What a shame! It has two broken legs!"

He laid the 24-hour-old baby pig outside the pig pen.

"Why did you put the baby pig outside the pen?" Linda asked.

"Its mother accidentally laid on it. It has two broken legs. One leg is almost two inches shorter than the other. It has two misplaced teeth that won't allow it to eat without biting itself. I must put it out of its misery," her father said.

"No, please, let me have it!"

Her father paused, "Well, alright, you can have it. You are 11, but you must take care of it every day. It is your responsibility. I cannot leave it in misery!"

Linda picked up the small baby piglet, took it into the house, and put it into a box with an old towel. She found an old eyedropper, warmed some milk, and fed the piglet which weighed less than a pound.

School was out, and for Linda, it was the end of the fifth grade. The teacher had been reading to the class the book entitled <u>Charlotte's Web</u> which is about a pig named Wilbur and a spider named Charlotte, so Linda decided to name the piglet 'Wilbur.'

Now, the physical therapy started for Wilbur. Since both back legs were broken, Linda decided to use saved popsicle sticks to set the legs. The breaks were clean ones, and the skin was not broken. She rubbed the short one with horse liniment, and taped the sticks to each of the legs. Every day, Wilbur got a warm bath, and both back legs were rubbed with more horse liniment. New popsicle sticks were taped back onto the legs.

Physical therapy continued with a warm bath, and the legs were rubbed early morning and late afternoon with more horse liniment. Popsicle sticks and new tape were applied daily. Linda's father was always checking to see that Wilbur was being cared for and fed as Wilbur was Linda's responsibility.

Wilbur's diet also improved. Linda cooked thin oatmeal and mixed it with butter and brown sugar. She fed Wilbur with a small spoon from her doll dishes. Wow! Wilbur loved that oatmeal-brown sugar mixture. In 14 days, Wilbur went from one pound to eight pounds.

Linda's mother said, "You have invested a fortune in oatmeal and brown sugar. Start weaning him."

After about two weeks, Linda put Wilbur on the chicken scale. Wilbur weighed 8 pounds, but was not yet walking.

Linda's mother, her grandfather, and Linda had to go to the field to cut thistles and milkweeds out of the soybeans. It was about 5:30 a.m., and the sun was just coming up. Before Linda left for the field, she put Wilbur in the shade of a tree. She didn't realize that the sun would turn to the west while she was working in the field. By the time she got back, Wilbur, a shiny, beautiful, Chester White pig, was badly sunburned. He had blisters all over. Petroleum jelly was applied to Wilbur's blisters. His ears were much worse than the rest of his body. By day two, the blisters had broken. More petroleum jelly was applied. By days five and six, he was peeling badly, and by day seven, he was healed.

**L**inda's mother again said, "You cannot keep feeding that pig all that brown sugar. Cut it back!"

Oatmeal with less brown sugar didn't work well. Wilbur felt a lot lighter. Back to the chicken scale. Wilbur had lost three pounds and now weighed five pounds.

L inda's grandpa saw Wilbur and said, "That pig will not be able to eat regular food. It has tusk teeth and is biting itself."

Before Linda could say anything, her grandpa grabbed Wilbur out of her arms. He pulled the tusk teeth with a pliers that he always carried with him. Oh, how Wilbur cried!! Grandpa's crude dentistry did help Wilbur.

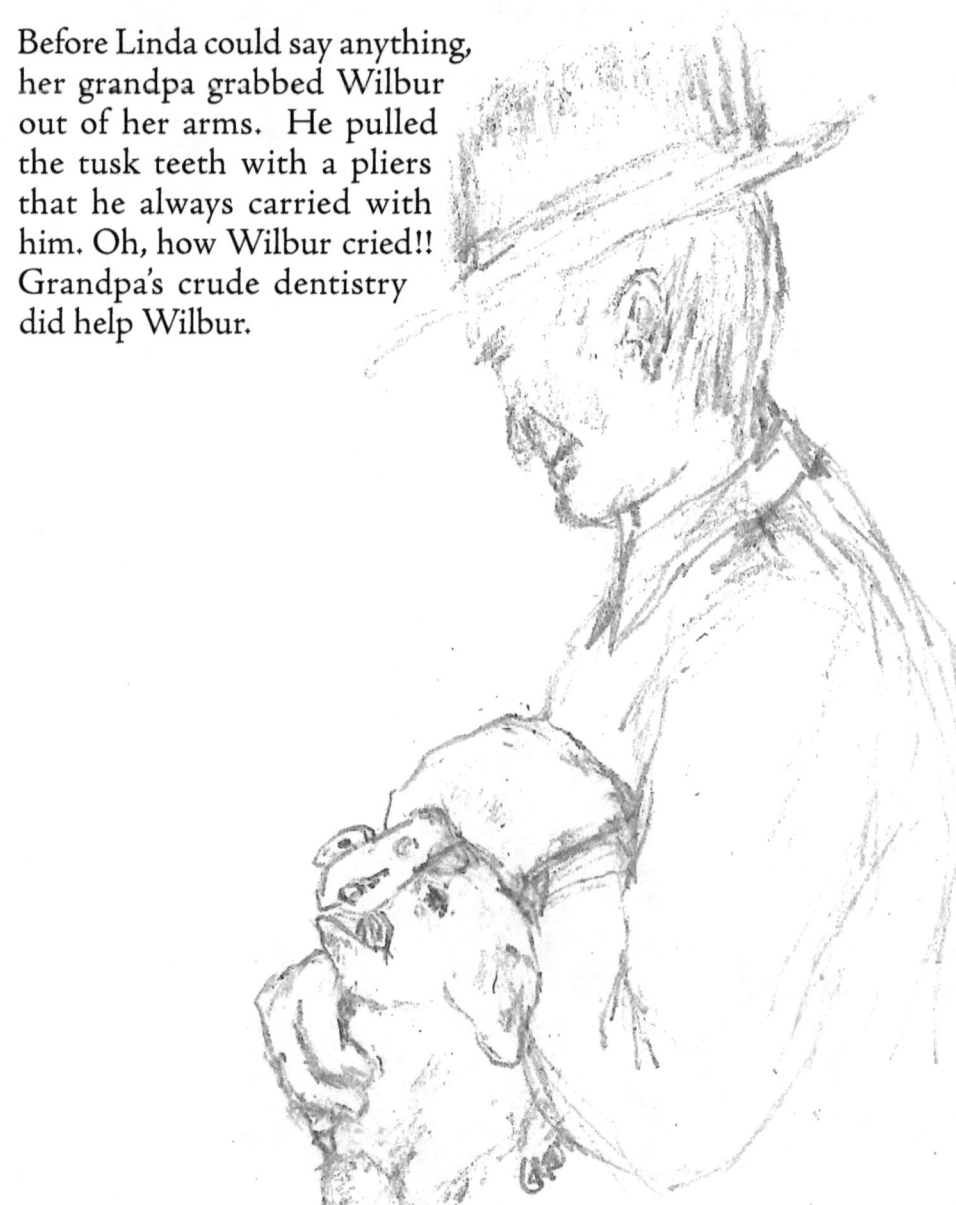

**W**ilbur's diet improved. Eating was easy now that the tusk teeth were gone. Daily physical therapy also continued without the popsicle sticks and tape. Wilbur took the first steps to a productive, new life: walking with Linda's help.

**P**hysical therapy was repeated every day. The one leg that was two inches shorter at birth had now developed into the same full-size of the other leg, and soon Wilbur was able to walk alone. Now, Wilbur was too big for the chicken scale, and was running instead of walking.

Wilbur didn't know that he was a pig. He thought that he was a dog. Wilbur was too small to be put in with the other pigs, so he had the run of the yard, along with the dog who seemed to look after Wilbur.

S ince it was fair time, Linda and her family decided to go to the fair.

When the family got home, there was no Wilbur to be found, just the dog. Had someone stolen Wilbur?

Linda often talked to Wilbur, so she called to him. Wilbur heard her, and made a soft "oink, oink" sound to let her know that he was OK. Wilbur had burrowed into the pile of corncob husks to keep warm. Oh, what a relief, Wilbur was safe!

Wilbur also thought that he was a chicken. He really loved the chicken food. Mamma chicken and her baby chicks did not like Wilbur as a roommate. That living arrangement didn't go well with daddy chicken either. There were a few pig-chicken arguments. Wilbur lost and moved out.

**W**ilbur was sure that the dog didn't really care that much about the doghouse, so Wilbur moved into the doghouse.

The tragedy occurred when a neighbor came over, pounded on the doghouse, and said, "Your dog looks like a pig."

Wilbur panicked, and in an attempt to get out, tore off the doghouse door frame. After that, Wilbur decided to move in with the other pigs and eat pig food.

One morning, Linda's father called her to come to the barn. She got a BIG surprise: Wilbur, that physically challenged, nearly dead pig, born with one leg shorter than the other, and both back legs broken, had become a mom. Wilbur had seven piglets. Oh, how great! This ends the story of a beautiful animal who became a success, even with many odds against her.

Moral: All people and animals have challenges to overcome. Wilbur, whose mother accidently laid on him, was born with one leg two inches shorter than the other and both back legs broken. Wilbur suffered a bad sunburn with large blisters over most of his body and tusk teeth that had to be pulled. She grew up to be a successful mother pig. You can overcome your challenges, too! Don't ever give up! Endurance, patience, faith, and love can heal many things!

By the way, this is a true story written to inspire children who are experiencing physical therapy and physical challenges.

# The End

www.ingramcontent.com/pod-product-compliance
Lightning Source LLC
LaVergne TN
LVHW041554060526
838200LV00037B/1283